KU-236-981

YOUR PASSPORT TO

SRI LANKA

>> by Nancy Dickmann >>

raintree 🗝

a Capstone company — publishers for children

Raintree is an imprint of Capstone Global Library Limited, a company incorporated in England and Wales having its registered office at 264 Banbury Road, Oxford, OX2 7DY – Registered company number: 6695582

www.raintree.co.uk
myorders@raintree.co.uk

Text © Capstone Global Library Limited 2022
The moral rights of the proprietor have been asserted.

All rights reserved. No part of this publication may be reproduced in any form or by any means (including photocopying or storing it in any medium by electronic means and whether or not transiently or incidentally to some other use of this publication) without the written permission of the copyright owner, except in accordance with the provisions of the Copyright, Designs and Patents Act 1988 or under the terms of a licence issued by the Copyright Licensing Agency, 5th Floor, Shackleton House, 4 Battle Bridge Lane, London SE1 2HX (www.cla.co.uk). Applications for the copyright owner's written permission should be addressed to the publisher.

Edited by Clare Lewis
Designed by Juliette Peters
Original illustrations © Capstone Global Library Limited 2022
Picture research by Tracy Cummins
Production by Laura Manthe
Originated by Capstone Global Library Ltd
Printed and bound in India

978 1 3982 1514 6 (hardback)
978 1 3982 1513 9 (paperback)

British Library Cataloguing in Publication Data
A full catalogue record for this book is available from the British Library.

Acknowledgements
We would like to thank the following for permission to reproduce photographs:
Capstone: Eric Gohl, 5; Dreamstime: Mitchell Gunn, 28; iStockphoto: hadynyah, 19; Newscom: REUTERS/Dinuka Liyanawatte, 25; Shutterstock: Aleksandar Todorovic, 11, DESIGNFACTS, 24, Epic_Sam, 14, givaga, cover, Guy Mace Photography, 23, Marius Dobilas, 7, piotreknik, 9, Rawpixel.com, 20, SamanWeeratunga, 27, SJ Travel Photo and Video, 13, Thomas Wyness, 17. Design elements: iStockphoto: Yevhenii Dubinko; Shutterstock: 10topvector, Flipser, MicroOne, N.Vector Design, pingebat.

Every effort has been made to contact copyright holders of material reproduced in this book. Any omissions will be rectified in subsequent printings if notice is given to the publisher.

All the internet addresses (URLs) given in this book were valid at the time of going to press. However, due to the dynamic nature of the internet, some addresses may have changed, or sites may have changed or ceased to exist since publication. While the author and publisher regret any inconvenience this may cause readers, no responsibility for any such changes can be accepted by either the author or the publisher.

CONTENTS

Words in **bold** are in the glossary.

CHAPTER ONE

WELCOME TO SRI LANKA!

The sun shines down on a beautiful beach. Clear turquoise water laps at the sand. Palm trees sway in the breeze. The water is full of surfers and swimmers. This is one of Sri Lanka's famous beaches. People come from all over the world to enjoy the sun and sand. But there is much more to this amazing country!

Sri Lanka is an island nation. The island is shaped like a teardrop. It lies in the Indian Ocean, just off the coast of India. Nearly 23 million people live in Sri Lanka. Sri Lanka has close links to India. But it has a culture and identity all its own.

MAP OF SRI LANKA

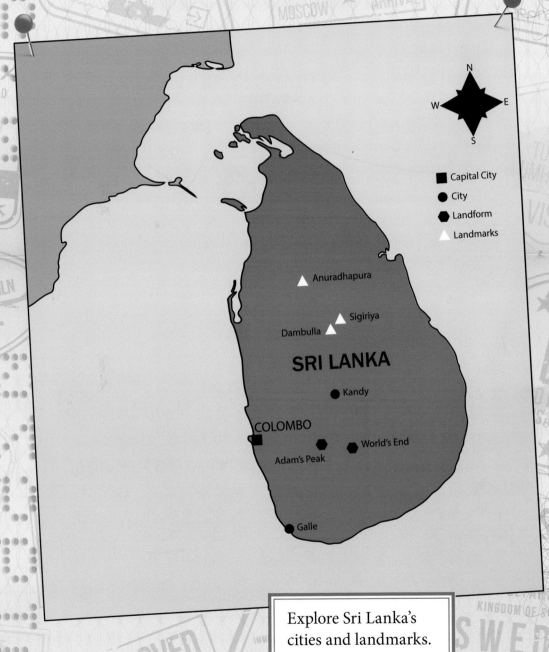

Capital City
City
Landform
Landmarks

Anuradhapura

Sigiriya

Dambulla

SRI LANKA

Kandy

COLOMBO

Adam's Peak

World's End

Galle

Explore Sri Lanka's cities and landmarks.

FACT FILE

OFFICIAL NAME: DEMOCRATIC SOCIALIST REPUBLIC OF SRI LANKA
POPULATION: 22,889,201
LAND AREA: 64,630 SQ KM (24,954 SQ. MI.)
CAPITALS: COLOMBO, SRI JAYEWARDENEPURA KOTTE
MONEY: SRI LANKAN RUPEE
GOVERNMENT: PRESIDENTIAL REPUBLIC
LANGUAGES: SINHALA AND TAMIL
GEOGRAPHY: Sri Lanka has a region of mountains in the central area, surrounded by flat or gently rolling plains.
NATURAL RESOURCES: Sri Lanka produces crops such as rice, tea, rubber and coconuts. Natural resources include gemstones, graphite and limestone.

DIFFERENT CULTURES

Sri Lanka's population is made up of different groups. The largest group is the Sinhalas. They are **indigenous** people of Sri Lanka. They make up about 75 per cent of the population. About 15 per cent are Tamils.

Sri Lanka's warm climate, delicious food and beautiful beaches make it popular with tourists.

Some groups of Tamils have lived in Sri Lanka for centuries. Others first came there from India between the 1840s and 1930s. About 9 per cent of Sri Lankans are Muslims. They came to the island centuries ago.

The different groups tend to live in separate areas. They often follow different religions. They speak their own languages and have their own traditions.

CHAPTER TWO

HISTORY OF SRI LANKA

OLD AND NEW

About 2,500 years ago, people began to arrive in Sri Lanka. They came from northern India. They set up Sri Lanka's first kingdom. It was centred around the city of Anuradhapura. People built **temples** and palaces. They also built systems to water crops.

THE FIRST SINHALAS

Sri Lankans tell a story about a prince called Vijaya. Vijaya's father banished him from India, so he and 700 others sailed to Sri Lanka. Legend says that he was the first person to arrive from India. Vijaya defeated the evil spirits who lived there and set up a peaceful kingdom.

There are many Buddhist shrines in Sri Lanka.

BUDDHISM

In about 250 BC, a new religion arrived. Buddhists from India visited Sri Lanka. They followed the teachings of the Buddha. He was a spiritual leader who founded the Buddhist religion. These people taught others about their religion. Many people soon started to follow **Buddhism**.

SHIPS AND TRADE

Sri Lanka was located on many trade routes. Sailors from Greece and Rome sometimes stopped there. So did ships from Arabia and China. People traded goods and shared ideas. In the 1500s, ships began arriving from Europe as well.

EUROPEANS ARRIVE

Fast ships arrived in Sri Lanka in 1505. They came from Portugal. The Portuguese began to trade in the region. Soon they built a fort. They took control of more of Sri Lanka. They traded cinnamon and elephants with other countries.

FACT

Historical records show that until the 1400s, you could walk from India to Sri Lanka. A path of limestone lies between the two. Most of it is now underwater.

TIMELINE OF SRI LANKAN HISTORY

ABOUT 380 BC: The first Sinhala capital is founded in Anuradhapura.

ABOUT 250 BC: The religion of Buddhism arrives in Sri Lanka.

1017: The capital of Sri Lanka moves to Polonnaruwa.

1505: Portuguese traders arrive in Sri Lanka and soon take over.

1658: The Dutch force the Portuguese out of Sri Lanka.

1796: The British take over Sri Lanka and name it Ceylon.

1948: Ceylon becomes an independent country.

1972: The country changes its name from Ceylon to Sri Lanka.

1983: A civil war between the Sinhala-led government of Sri Lanka and Tamil groups begins.

2009: The civil war ends with a government victory.

Some buildings from the British period can still be seen today.

By 1658 the Dutch had forced the Portuguese out. The Dutch ruled Sri Lanka for more than a century. Then, in 1796, the British took over. They named the country Ceylon.

INDEPENDENCE AND WAR

By the 20th century, Sri Lankans wanted to govern themselves. They finally became **independent** in 1948. But not everyone was happy. The Tamils wanted to be separate. A **civil war** began in 1983. It lasted until 2009.

CHAPTER THREE

EXPLORE SRI LANKA

For a fairly small island, Sri Lanka packs a lot in. The beautiful mountains are covered in trees and greenery. The tallest is known as Sri Pada, or Adam's Peak. The region has deep valleys and steep cliffs. One cliff is known as World's End. It is about 1,220 metres (4,000 feet) high.

The rest of Sri Lanka's land slopes gradually down to the sea. There are hot and humid **rainforests**. There are also **grasslands** and farms. Sri Lanka has a rainy season each year. It is called the monsoon.

FACT

The top of Sri Pada mountain is flat. There is a hollow in the rock that looks like a footprint. "Sri Pada" means "holy footprint". Buddhists believe that it was made by the Buddha. Muslims and Christians believe it was made by Adam, the first man in the Bible.

By law, elephants are protected from hunters in Sri Lanka.

AMAZING ANIMALS

Many people visit Sri Lanka to see wildlife. There are large herds of elephants. Leopards slink through the forests. Brightly coloured birds fill the trees. Off the coast, there are whales and dolphins.

Sri Lanka has many bell-shaped structures called stupas. They are holy sites for Buddhists.

ANCIENT SITES

Sri Lanka has many historic sites. One of the most famous is Anuradhapura. This city was built thousands of years ago. It was abandoned around AD 1000. Then it was covered over by jungle. Some of its buildings are still standing. There are temples and pools. Buddhist ceremonies are still held here.

Dambulla is another Buddhist site. It is made up of five caves. Long ago, people built temples in the caves. There are many statues of the Buddha. There are beautiful paintings on the walls.

BUDDHISM IN SRI LANKA

Buddhists follow the teachings of a man known as the Buddha. Buddhists believe that, long ago, he sat under a fig tree to think. He wanted to find answers about life. There is a very old tree in Anuradhapura. It is said to have grown from a cutting of the Buddha's fig tree. It is a holy site for Buddhists.

THE LION ROCK

Sigiriya is in central Sri Lanka. A huge, steep rock towers over the plains. At the top is a **fortress**. A king built it in the late 400s. A huge stone lion once guarded the path to it. Only its feet remain now. Visitors must pass between them to climb to the top.

EXCITING CITIES

Colombo is Sri Lanka's largest city. It is on the island's southwest coast. Ships from many lands once docked in its **harbour**. It is still an important port today. Tourists walk along the city's shady avenues. Many of the buildings date from the time of British rule.

Galle is on the southern coast. The Portuguese used it as their main trading port. The Dutch later built a fort there. The city has many historic buildings. Tourists visit restaurants to try fresh seafood. There are markets, shops and food stalls.

KANDY

Kandy lies in the forested hills at the heart of the island. It was once the capital of its own kingdom. It still has a vibrant and unique culture. Tourists come to watch colourful parades and festivals. Its name comes from *kanda*, the Sinhala word for *hill*.

In Kandy, drummers play as people perform traditional dances.

CHAPTER FOUR

DAILY LIFE

In Sri Lanka, fewer than 20 per cent of people live in cities. The rest live in the countryside. In the cities, many people get around in tuk-tuks. These three-wheeled vehicles are often brightly painted. They are used as taxis. People also sell food from them and make deliveries. Trains connect the island's cities and towns.

EDUCATION

Education is very important in Sri Lanka. About 92 per cent of Sri Lankans are able to read. School is free, and most children attend. The school day often starts early. The youngest children only have a few hours of school each day. Older children stay for longer periods.

Most Sri Lankan children wear school uniforms.

Tea is often planted on hillsides so the soil doesn't get too soggy.

GROWING TEA

Many people in the central highlands work on large tea farms. In Sri Lanka, tea leaves are usually picked by hand. This is very hard work. Pickers often work long hours for little pay. Many tea workers live on the plantations. Their families live with them.

RELIGION

Religion plays a large role in Sri Lankan life. About 70 per cent of the population is Buddhist. This includes most of the Sinhala people. Many young men and women become Buddhist monks or nuns.

The Tamils are mainly Hindu. There are also many Muslims and Christians. However, in Sri Lanka, the faiths sometimes mix. Some Buddhist temples have statues of Hindu gods. People of all faiths take part in each other's festivals.

LANGUAGES OF SRI LANKA

Sri Lanka has two official languages: Sinhala and Tamil. They are written using different systems. About 75 per cent of the population speaks Sinhala. Most of the rest speak Tamil. A few people still speak a language based on Portuguese. It was once used across the country. About 25 per cent of the population speaks English as a foreign language.

CURRY

Traders from many lands visited Sri Lanka in the past. They all had an influence on its food. It now reflects a mix of different cultures. Sri Lanka is especially famous for curries. These spicy stews are served with rice. In Sri Lanka, they are often made with fish. They can also be based on meat, lentils or vegetables.

STREET FOOD

Many people buy fast food from street stalls. Kottu roti is a very popular dish. It uses leftover roti, a flatbread, cut into strips. The flatbread is mixed with vegetables, meat and spices. Then everything is stir-fried. Hoppers are also popular. These are pancakes made from rice flour and coconut milk. They are cooked in a bowl shape. A fried egg is often cooked inside.

GODAMBA ROTI

These flatbreads are common in Sri Lanka. They can be served plain alongside a curry or wrapped around a savoury filling.

Ingredients:
- 450 grams plain flour
- 480–720 ml vegetable oil
- salt for seasoning
- water

Instructions:

1. Put the flour, salt and 3 tablespoons of oil in a large bowl and mix them together.
2. Add water, a little bit at a time, until you have a soft dough. If it is too wet, add more flour.
3. Knead the dough for about 10 minutes.
4. Divide the dough into balls, slightly larger than a golf ball.
5. Put the balls into a shallow dish and add oil until they are completely covered. Cover it with a dish towel and leave for at least 6 hours.
6. Take a ball from the oil and use your hands to stretch and flatten it into a thin pancake.
7. Ask an adult to help you heat a wok or large frying pan. Fry the roti for about 30 seconds on each side.
8. Repeat steps 6 and 7 with the rest of the balls.

CHAPTER FIVE

HOLIDAYS AND CELEBRATIONS

The calendar in Sri Lanka is packed with colourful festivals. Most are related to one of the island's religions. Sri Lankans celebrate the New Year in April. People get ready by cleaning and painting their homes. They buy new clothes.

During this holiday you hear the sound of firecrackers and drums. Families share special meals. They also exchange gifts. They give offerings to the gods. People gather in the streets to play games.

These sweet treats are popular at New Year celebrations.

Families often gather to watch the pongal cooking.

HARVEST FESTIVAL

In January, Tamils celebrate the rice harvest. This four-day festival is called Thai Pongal. It also celebrates the longer days that spring will bring. People cook a special dish called *pongal*. It is made of rice, milk, sugar, nuts and raisins. If the cooking pot overflows, this is thought to bring good luck.

CELEBRATING BUDDHA

The festival of Vesak Poya takes place in May. It always starts on a full moon. Sinhalas celebrate the life of the Buddha. People visit the temple to **meditate**. There are parades with colourful lanterns.

Esala Perahera takes place in Kandy. A temple there is said to hold one of the Buddha's teeth. The festival honours this sacred tooth. It also honours Hindu gods. Thousands of people come to watch the parade. There are elephants dressed in colourful fabrics. One of them carries the tooth. There are acrobats, jugglers, dancers and musicians.

FACT

Sri Lankans celebrate their independence from Britain each year on 4 February. There are speeches and parades. People sing the national anthem as the flag is raised.

The Esala Perahera celebrations are full of colour and music.

CHAPTER SIX

SPORT AND RECREATION

Cricket is the most popular sport in Sri Lanka. Many people also play **amateur** cricket. Crowds gather to watch professional matches. They are played around the island. The national team is one of the best in the world. They won the World Cup in 1996.

Many people think that Kumar Sangakkara was one of the best cricketers ever.

OTHER SPORTS

Volleyball is the official national sport of Sri Lanka. Many people play this game. They also play beach volleyball. This version is played on sand by teams of two. Sri Lankans also enjoy football, rugby, badminton and netball.

KANAA ALLEEMA

This is a popular children's game. It is often played as part of the New Year celebrations by adults as well as children. You need a large group of people, a big open space and a blindfold.

1. Use chalk or another method to mark out a large circle on the ground.
2. Choose one person to be "it" and blindfold them.
3. The person who is "it" must try to tag the other players.
4. Anyone who is tagged or runs outside the circle is out.
5. If the blindfolded person runs out of the circle, someone guides them back in.
6. The last person who hasn't been caught is the winner.

GLOSSARY

amateur
done for fun rather than as
a job

Buddhism
religion based on following
the teachings of the man
known as the Buddha

civil war
war fought between
different groups within
a country, rather than
between different countries

fortress
structure that is built to
defend against attack

grassland
large area of land with
grasses but few trees

harbour
body of water along a coast
that provides a safe place
for ships to dock

independent
not ruled over by
anyone else

indigenous
native to a place

meditate
relax the mind and body by
thinking quietly and deeply

rainforest
type of thick, dense forest
that receives a lot of rain

temple
sacred building where
religious rituals take place

FIND OUT MORE

BOOKS

Celebrating Buddhist Festivals (Celebration Days),
Nick Hunter (Raintree, 2016)

Introducing Asia (Introducing Continents),
Anita Ganeri (Raintree, 2013)

*Our World in Pictures: Countries, Cultures, People and
Places: A Visual Encyclopedia of the World*, DK
(DK Children, 2020)

WEBSITES

www.bbc.co.uk/bitesize/topics/zh4mrj6/articles/zdbvjhv
Learn more about Buddhism.

www.dkfindout.com/uk/earth/continents/asia
Find out more about Asia.

INDEX

OTHER BOOKS IN THIS SERIES

YOUR PASSPORT TO ARGENTINA

YOUR PASSPORT TO CHINA

YOUR PASSPORT TO ECUADOR

YOUR PASSPORT TO EL SALVADOR

YOUR PASSPORT TO ETHIOPIA

YOUR PASSPORT TO FRANCE

YOUR PASSPORT TO GUATEMALA

YOUR PASSPORT TO IRAN

YOUR PASSPORT TO ITALY

YOUR PASSPORT TO KENYA

YOUR PASSPORT TO PERU

YOUR PASSPORT TO RUSSIA

YOUR PASSPORT TO SOUTH KOREA

YOUR PASSPORT TO SPAIN

YOUR PASSPORT TO SRI LANKA

YOUR PASSPORT TO TURKEY